Scholdeners

NUMBER TRACING

This book belongs to an awesome kid called

Available now on Amazon

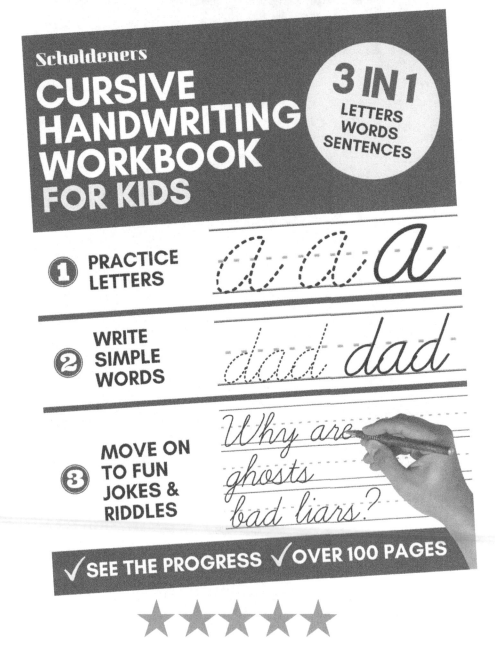

The Most Fun, Engaging & Comprehensive Way To Learn Cursive Handwriting

- 110 pages – with more than 100 pages of writing exercises
- This 3-in-1 workbook will gently guide the child from beginner until they are happy and confidently writing sentences

Indroduction & Tips

Learning numeracy for the first time should be a fun and exciting journey for a child, but it can also be a little daunting. To make the process as smooth and effective as possible, here are ten top tips:

1. Body basics
Good posture is important for any writing. Encourage children to sit with their feet flat on the floor, their back straight (no heads on the table) and relaxed shoulders.

2. Think Ink
Although children usually write in pencil at school, it can be useful for them to start out with felt tips and gel pens, which have a nice, fluid delivery of ink.

3. B prepared
If your child is using a pencil, the softer B pencils are generally easier to write with as they move more fluently across the page.

4. Let loose
Don't stick to practising on paper. Get children to practise their numbers in other mediums, such as tracing them in the air, in sand with a stick or on another person's back with their finger. Make learning fun and creative.

5. Get a grip
Keep an eye on the child's pencil grip. It's important that the pad of the thumb connects with the pencil. If the side or tip of the thumb touches, it closes up the hand and restricts the flow of movement.

6. Let's twist

Your child may find writing easier if their paper is turned at an angle. You can turn the page up to 45 degrees in either direction.

7. Left learning

Left-handed children may have more trouble as they push the pencil across the paper, rather than pulling it. A writing slope can be beneficial for left-handed children as it helps them to see their writing.

8. Teaching terms

To help your child at home, ask how numeracy is being taught at school: for example, do they form their numbers in certain ways? It's important to use consistent styles so you can give your child effective instructions.

9. Method matching

Handwriting styles vary from school to school, so it's important to be consistent and ask children to write 'f's, 'r's, 'k's and other letters that tend to vary in style the same way at home and in the classroom.

10. Easy does it

Finally, keep numeracy practice light and fun. Nagging your child about their progress will only reduce their enthusiasm. Always give praise where it's due and try not to hover over them – they need time to fully experience each task.

Now we have a few pointers, let's begin . . .

I have __1__ robot

one

Let's write ↓1

one one one one

Do you remember?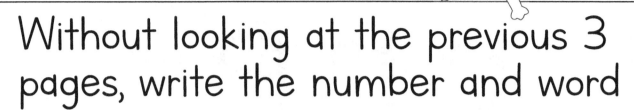

Without looking at the previous 3 pages, write the number and word

number

word

AWESOME WORK - YOU ARE A ★

I have **2** dinosaurs

two

Let's write 2

2 2 2 2 2 2 2 2

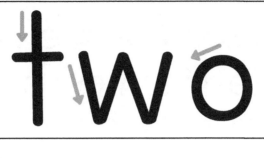

two two two two

Do you remember?

Without looking at the previous 3 pages, write the number and word

| number |

| word |

I have 3 planes

three

Let's write 3

3 3 3 3 3 3 3 3

1 2 **3** 4 5 6 7 8 9 10 11 12 13 14 15 16 17 18 19 20

three

three three three

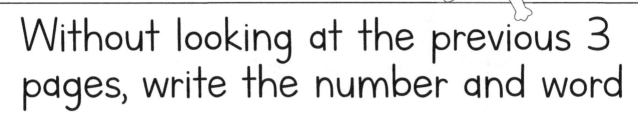

Do you remember?

Without looking at the previous 3 pages, write the number and word

number

word

I have 4 kites

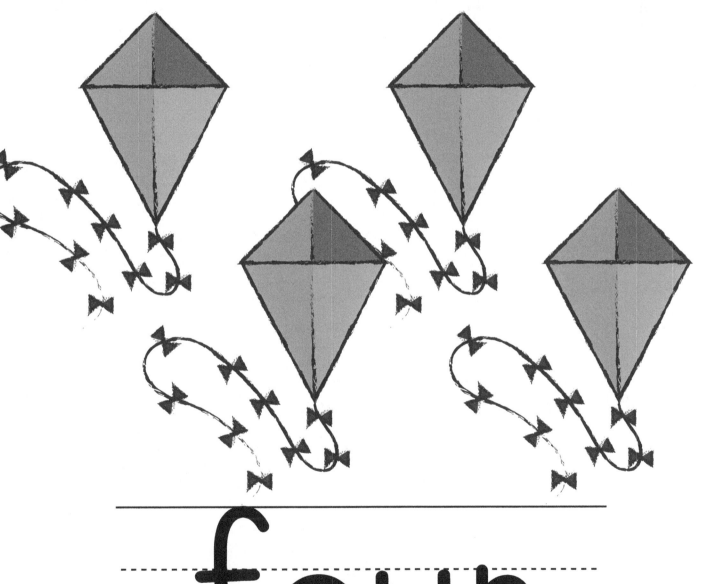

four

1 2 3 **4** 5 6 7 8 9 10 11 12 13 14 15 16 17 18 19 20

Let's write 4

four

four four four four

Do you remember?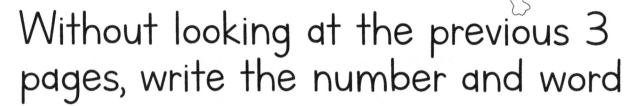

Without looking at the previous 3 pages, write the number and word

number

word

YOU JUST GET BETTER AND BETTER ✓

1 2 3 4 **5** 6 7 8 9 10 11 12 13 14 15 16 17 18 19 20

I have 5 bunnies

five

Let's write 5

5 5 5 5 5 5 5 5

five five five five

Do you remember?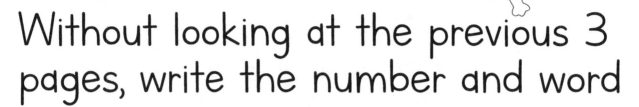

Without looking at the previous 3 pages, write the number and word

number

word

YOU DESERVE A HIGH (YOU KNOW THE NUMBER!)

I have 6 trees

six

Let's write 6

6 6 6 6 6 6 6 6

1 2 3 4 5 **6** 7 8 9 10 11 12 13 14 15 16 17 18 19 20

six

six six six six six six

Do you remember?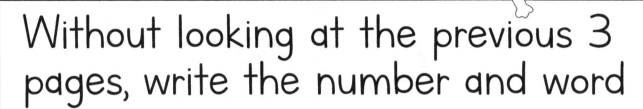

Without looking at the previous 3 pages, write the number and word

number

word

1 2 3 4 5 6 **7** 8 9 10 11 12 13 14 15 16 17 18 19 20

I have 7 apples

seven

Let's write 7

7 7 7 7 7 7 7 7 7

1 2 3 4 5 6 **7** 8 9 10 11 12 13 14 15 16 17 18 19 20

seven

seven seven seven

Do you remember?

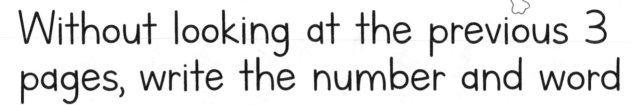

Without looking at the previous 3 pages, write the number and word

number _____

_____

_____

_____

word _____

_____

_____

_____

I have 8 owls

eight

1 2 3 4 5 6 7 **8** 9 10 11 12 13 14 15 16 17 18 19 20

Let's write 8

8 8 8 8 8 8 8 8

eight　　eight　　eight

Do you remember?

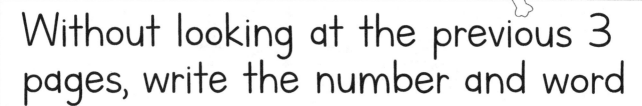

Without looking at the previous 3 pages, write the number and word

number

word

1 2 3 4 5 6 7 8 **9** 10 11 12 13 14 15 16 17 18 19 20

I have **9** pencils

nine

1 2 3 4 5 6 7 8 **9** 10 11 12 13 14 15 16 17 18 19 20

Let's write q

q q q q q q q q q

nine

nine nine nine nine

Do you remember?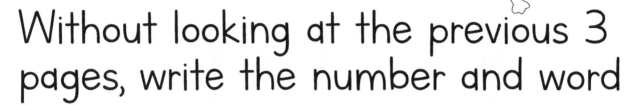

Without looking at the previous 3 pages, write the number and word

number

word

YOU'RE ONE SMART COOKIE

I have 10 books

ten

1 2 3 4 5 6 7 8 9 **10** 11 12 13 14 15 16 17 18 19 20

Let's write 10

10 10 10 10 10 10 10

1 2 3 4 5 6 7 8 9 **10** 11 12 13 14 15 16 17 18 19 20

ten ten ten ten ten

Do you remember?

> Without looking at the previous 3 pages, write the number and word

number	

word	

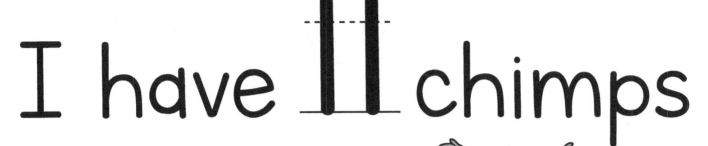

I have 11 chimps

eleven

Let's write 11

1 2 3 4 5 6 7 8 9 10 11 12 13 14 15 16 17 18 19 20

eleven

eleven eleven eleven

Do you remember?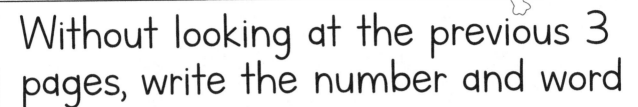

Without looking at the previous 3 pages, write the number and word

number

word

I have 12 balls

twelve

Let's write 12

12 12 12 12 12 12 12

1 2 3 4 5 6 7 8 9 10 11 **12** 13 14 15 16 17 18 19 20

twelve

twelve twelve twelve

Do you remember?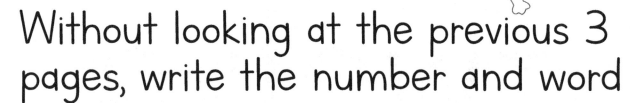

Without looking at the previous 3 pages, write the number and word

number

word

1 2 3 4 5 6 7 8 9 10 11 12 **13** 14 15 16 17 18 19 20

I have 13 cats

thirteen

Let's write 13

13 13 13 13 13 13 13

thirteen

thirteen thirteen

Do you remember?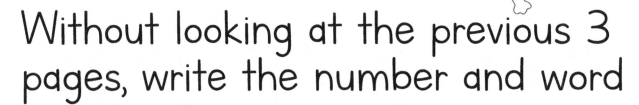

Without looking at the previous 3 pages, write the number and word

number

word

1 2 3 4 5 6 7 8 9 10 11 12 13 **14** 15 16 17 18 19 20

I have 14 balloons

fourteen

Let's write 14

fourteen

fourteen fourteen

Do you remember?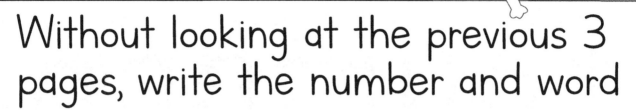

Without looking at the previous 3 pages, write the number and word

number

word

EVEN SANTA IS IMPRESSED

I have 15 drums

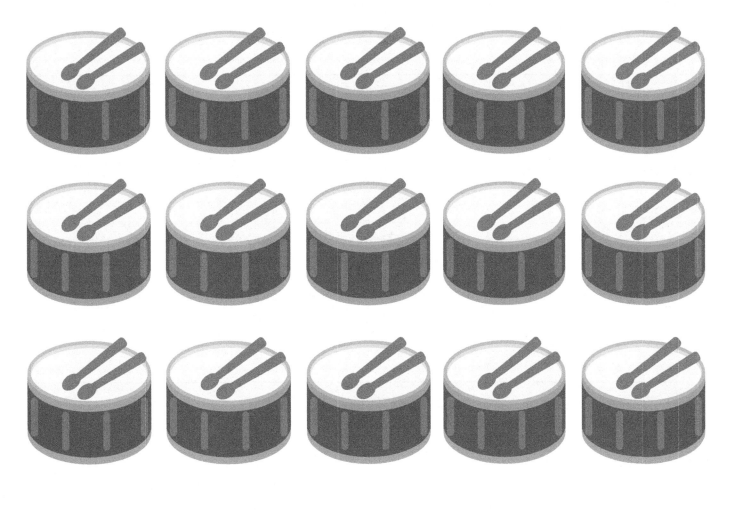

fifteen

Let's write 15

15 15 15 15 15 15 15

fifteen

fifteen fifteen fifteen

Do you remember?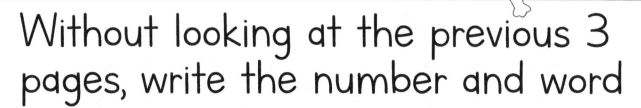

Without looking at the previous 3 pages, write the number and word

number

word

YOU TOTALLY ROCK!

1 2 3 4 5 6 7 8 9 10 11 12 13 14 15 **16** 17 18 19 20

I have 16 pandas

sixteen

Let's write 16

16 16 16 16 16 16 16

sixteen

sixteen sixteen sixteen

Do you remember?

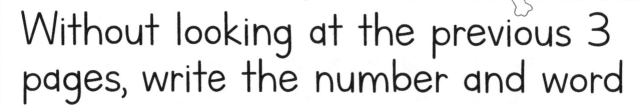

Without looking at the previous 3 pages, write the number and word

| number |

| word |

1 2 3 4 5 6 7 8 9 10 11 12 13 14 15 16 **17** 18 19 20

I have 17 guitars

seventeen

1 2 3 4 5 6 7 8 9 10 11 12 13 14 15 16 **17** 18 19 20

Let's write 17

17 17 17 17 17 17 17 17

1 2 3 4 5 6 7 8 9 10 11 12 13 14 15 16 **17** 18 19 20

seventeen

seventeen seventeen

Do you remember?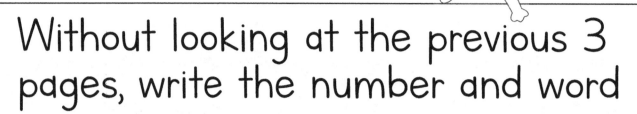

Without looking at the previous 3 pages, write the number and word

number

word

I have 18 lions

eighteen

Let's write 18

18   18   18   18   18   18   18

eighteen

eighteen eighteen

Do you remember?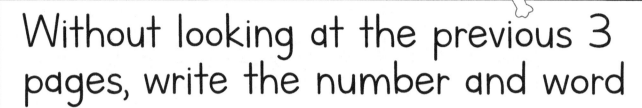

Without looking at the previous 3 pages, write the number and word

number

word

YOU'RE ON FIRE

1 2 3 4 5 6 7 8 9 10 11 12 13 14 15 16 17 18 **19** 20

I have fish

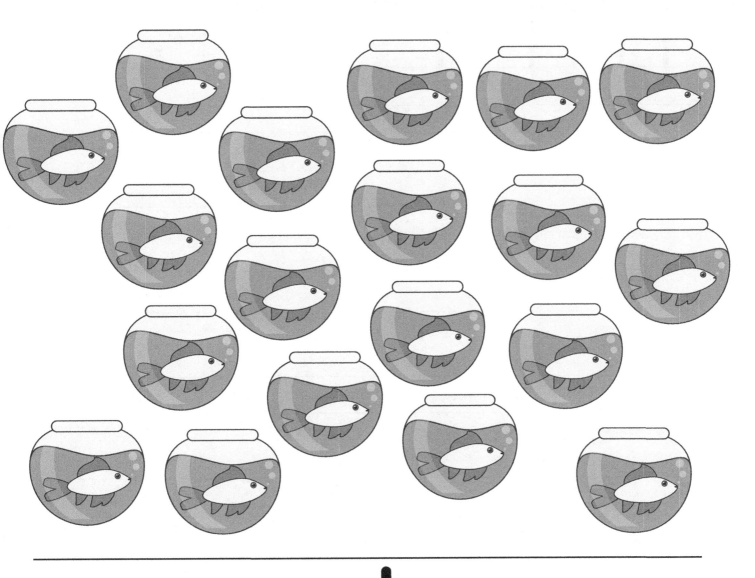

nineteen

1 2 3 4 5 6 7 8 9 10 11 12 13 14 15 16 17 18 **19** 20

Let's write 19

19 19 19 19 19 19 19 19 19

nineteen

nineteen nineteen

Do you remember?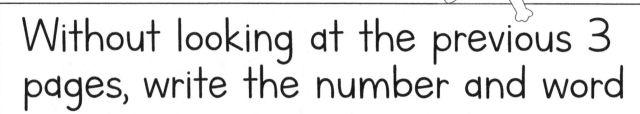

Without looking at the previous 3 pages, write the number and word

| number |

| word |

THAT'S ONE CLEVER KID

1 2 3 4 5 6 7 8 9 10 11 12 13 14 15 16 17 18 19 **20**

I have 20 dogs

twenty

Let's write 20

20 20 20 20 20 20 20

twenty

twenty twenty twenty

Do you remember?

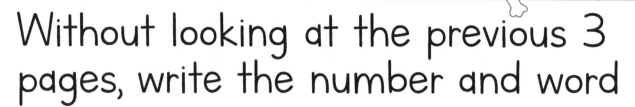

Without looking at the previous 3 pages, write the number and word

number

word

FIRST PRIZE GOES TO YOU

AWESOME WORK!

You have done brilliantly with your number writing - we couldn't be more proud of you!

Give yourself a huge pat on the back and ask mom or dad for a special treat - tell them the book said they had to!

EASY MATH

We are mightily impressed with how well you've done so far.

In fact, you're so good we think you can easily do some simple math.

Let's start with addition . . .

Easy Addition

Addition is bringing two or more numbers (or things) together to make a new total

$$1 + 2 = 3$$

Here, 1 circle is added to 2 other circles to make a total of 3 circles

Let's look at a few more examples . . .

Easy Addition

$1 + 3 = 4$

o   ooo   ooo o

$2 + 1 = 3$

oo   o   ooo

$3 + 2 = 5$

ooo   oo   ooo oo

Easy Addition

1 + 4 = 5

6 + 3 = 9

Now you try ➡

Easy Addition

1 + 1 = ☐

2 + 1 = ☐

3 + 2 = ☐

Easy Addition

4 + 2 =

2 + 2 =

3 + 3 =

Easy Addition

Let's take away the circles

2 + 1 = ☐

4 + 1 = ☐

3 + 2 = ☐

Easy Addition

Let's take away the circles

3 + 3 = ☐

4 + 2 = ☐

3 + 4 = ☐

Easy Addition

Let's take away the circles

$$3 + 5 = \boxed{}$$

$$5 + 4 = \boxed{}$$

$$4 + 4 = \boxed{}$$

Easy Addition

These ones are tough!

6 + 5 = ☐

7 + 6 = ☐

8 + 3 = ☐

Easy Addition

These are super tough!

$8 + 12 =$ ⬜

$10 + 11 =$ ⬜

$12 + 9 =$ ⬜

Easy Subtraction

Subtraction is the opposite of addition. You take one number away from another

$$3 - 2 = 1$$

Here, we start with 3 circles and then take 2 away, which leaves us with just 1 circle

Let's look at a few more examples . . .

Easy Subtraction

$$2 - 1 = 1$$

$$3 - 1 = 2$$

$$4 - 2 = 2$$

5 - 2 = 3

6 - 3 = 3

Now you try ➡

Easy Subtraction

2 - 1 = ☐

3 - 2 = ☐

4 - 2 = ☐

Easy Subtraction

$5 - 1 = \boxed{}$

$6 - 3 = \boxed{}$

$6 - 5 = \boxed{}$

Easy Subtraction

Let's take away the circles

3 - 1 = ☐

4 - 3 = ☐

5 - 1 = ☐

Easy Subtraction

Let's take away the circles

6 - 3 = ☐

7 - 5 = ☐

8 - 2 = ☐

Easy Subtraction

Let's take away the circles

9 - 5 = ☐

7 - 4 = ☐

6 - 2 = ☐

Easy Subtraction

These ones are tough!

$$10 - 4 = \boxed{}$$

$$12 - 3 = \boxed{}$$

$$14 - 7 = \boxed{}$$

Easy Subtraction

These are super tough!

$$12 - 11 = \boxed{}$$

$$15 - 12 = \boxed{}$$

$$18 - 14 = \boxed{}$$

Do you remember?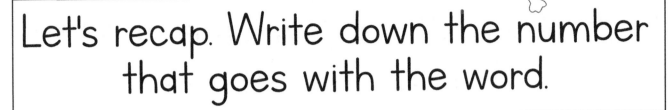

Let's recap. Write down the number that goes with the word.

Eighteen	Two
Twelve	Six
One	Seventeen

Do you remember?

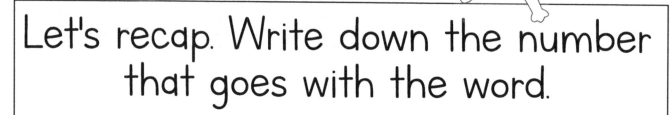

Let's recap. Write down the number that goes with the word.

Twenty	Fourteen
Five	Seven
Nineteen	Three

Sixteen	Eight
Four	Thirteen
Nine	Fifteen
Eleven	Ten

You are Number 1 in our book for reaching the end!

Keep learning, keep exploring

Made in United States
North Haven, CT
01 August 2022

22125471R00063